# Beyond
## Stitch *& Bitch*

### Reflections on Knitting and Life

# Beyond
## Stitch & *Bitch*

### Reflections on Knitting and Life

AFI-ODELIA E. SCRUGGS

BEYOND
WORDS
*Publishing*
I   N   C

Beyond Words Publishing, Inc.
20827 N.W. Cornell Road, Suite 500
Hillsboro, Oregon 97124-9808
503-531-8700

Previous versions of the following essays first appeared in the *Plain Dealer*:
Elizabeth Zimmermann: Mother of the Craft; Sometimes Knitters Are
So Lucky; and Redemption.

Editor: Jenefer Angell
Managing Editor: Beth Caldwell Hoyt
Proofreader: Jade Chan
Design: Jerry Soga
Composition: William H. Brunson Typography Services
Cover Design: Alexandra Graham

Printed in the United States of America
Distributed to the book trade by Publishers Group West

Library of Congress Control Number: 200410475

The corporate mission of Beyond Words Publishing, Inc.:
  *Inspire to Integrity*

# Contents

# Contents

# Acknowledgements

Writing is a solitary process, but producing a book is collaborative. The birth of an idea brings forth a community that grows larger and larger until the finished volume appears in stores.

I'd like to thank my agent, Janell, who has proven her faith in and dedication to this idea. I'd also like to thank the staff at Beyond Words Publishing, who picked up this book so quickly. All of you have been wonderful, but I want to single out Jenefer, my editor, who spoke softly while she cracked the whip.

There are other people who, though not intimately connected with this book, played a significant role in its publication. Thank you, Bakari, for sitting and watching me knit when you could have been playing with your brother and sister. Thank you, Sapriya and Max, for evenings long ago when I knit while you shared your elementary school adventures with me.

And most importantly, thanks to Mrs. Elizabeth Duncan, the woman who taught her class how to manipulate needles and yarn. Without you, none of this would have been possible.

# *Introduction*

I used to think that I couldn't meditate. Whenever I tried, I failed. All the books I read gave the same directions, and I followed them to the letter. They advised finding a comfortable position, so I pulled out a huge towel and spread it on the carpet. Then I turned on the electric radiator—my substitute for a fireplace—and placed it close enough to warm me, but far enough to keep from getting burned. I sat on my butt and straightened my back. I crossed my legs, placed my hands on my thighs, and closed my eyes.

And I waited.

I felt the rise and fall of my chest. I expanded my lungs as I inhaled and contracted my diaphragm as I exhaled. As my pulse slowed and my breaths deepened, I came to a realization.

My legs ached. So did my back. I wasn't two minutes into my session and my body had rebelled. My spine defied my attempts to keep it straight and settled into a slump. I had the distinct impression that some imp was running around me, sticking pins into my toes and the soles of my feet. The sensation disappeared only when my limbs turned to lead.

"Don't concentrate on the discomfort," I told myself. "Put your attention somewhere else."

Yeah, right. The imp had jumped from my feet to my head and had somehow entered my brain. Perhaps it had hitched a ride on a breath and had gotten off inside me before I exhaled.

My thoughts were out of control, rocking and rolling over each other.

"Ouch! Your feet hurt! You're hungry; can't you hear your stomach growling? That leftover slice of pizza would taste great right now.

"The only thing better than cold pizza is leftover spaghetti. Remember that slumber party you had when you were in the tenth grade? The one where Pam lit a candle for the séance under your mom's new dining room table? When your mom found out, she accused you of trying to burn down her house and declared an immediate ban on any future slumber parties. You all stayed up talking all night and ate cold spaghetti for breakfast the next morning.

"Pam moved to New York and died of cancer real young. Wonder what happened to the others . . ."

Frustrated, I admitted defeat. I stretched my legs, opened my eyes, and looked at the clock. My meditation session hadn't lasted ten minutes. I felt like I always felt after meditation: restless, not rested, and guilty over my inability to transcend mundane concerns and obligations. So I shook my head and did what I always did: I reached for my yarn and knitting needles.

I cast on forty, fifty, then 120 stitches, counting by twos several times to make sure I had the correct number. Counting became a chant as I concentrated on the loops of yarn sliding through my fingers.

My thoughts quieted down. The imp disappeared. The small movement of my hands and fingers revived my limbs, and my body regained a sense of itself. My spine wasn't straight and my toes still tingled, but they didn't distract me; they reminded me of the moment. I was moving. I was working. I was meditating, as surely as if I'd sat zazen for hours.

Now that I know a bit more about meditation, I understand why my earlier attempts were so unsuccessful. I was attempting to create a contemplative atmosphere instead of letting one unfold—like I do when I knit. Knitting brings me great peace and joy. I know, in part, that the craft appeals to my Protestant work ethic. My labor yields a tangible and, more importantly, useful product: a hat for winter, a blanket to huddle or cuddle under. My love touches someone even when I cannot.

But my appreciation of knitting has grown more profound as I consider all I've learned from it: patience, creativity, discipline, and diligence. Knitting is, quite simply, a spiritual practice. It's not the same as bowing one's head or folding one's hands and making a conscious effort to connect with the presence of the Divine, but when one knits, especially if one concentrates on the work in one's hands, the conscious self gets out of the way. Maybe it takes a well-deserved rest; maybe it actually vacates the body and hovers close by. Lord knows it rarely gets a break from the daily routine.

The important thing is this: when the conscious retreats, the Divine presence can advance. We connect with God for a minute, or less. The length of time isn't as essential as the strengthening of the connection.

This insight came gradually, after contemplating a number of church sermons. But the incident that opened the way still shines in my memory. It occurred years ago, and I wasn't in church at all. I was driving home to see my family after many years away. I was happy and excited, not only at the chance to be with my relatives, but at the turns my life had taken. I'd settled on a career in journalism and was working at a daily newspaper. Sure, the job was only a summer internship—and I was a good ten years older than the other interns—but I was confident that this opportunity would lead to others. For once it seemed I was headed in the right direction.

I would have made the five-hour drive without a break, but my bladder wouldn't stay on schedule. So I gave in and turned into a rest stop. On the way out of the building, I picked up a brochure about Kentucky's Shaker Village.

The sect is known for the quality of its crafts. Shaker cloaks are warm and durable. Shaker chairs have outlasted the communities that produced them. The brochure was filled with glossy photographs, but their allure wasn't due to the photographer's expertise. Every picture had a presence because the Shakers worked as if God would enjoy the fruit of their labors. God would sit in their chairs. God would step on their rugs. God would pick up their brooms and sweep the dust from Heaven's floors.

I thought about the Shakers while driving. What if I were knitting for God, instead of for fulfillment or out of necessity? What would I think about while I worked? Would I curse when I dropped a stitch?

(Come on, we all mutter a word or two when we're picking up stitches.) Over the years, I've asked a different question: If I were knitting for God, what exactly was I making? Was it a hat or a potential blessing? I chose the latter; it made me happier.

Collectively, these thoughts have led me to knit with a different focus. Yes, I'm making a practical item. That goal keeps me going strong, but I trust that the intelligence in my fingers will get the work done flawlessly. I let my mind wander away from stitches, rows, and repeats to consider the other, higher purpose of my work.

I think about the way knitting connects me to my fourth-grade teacher, who taught the craft to her eager class, and how small lessons endure for a life-time. I remember how the threat of serious illness kindled my still-unfulfilled desire to share my love for knitting with another. I think about the way knitting has traditionally represented industry and productivity, and my thoughts turn to inmates at the Ohio Reformatory for Women who use knitting and other needlecrafts to repay their debts to society.

I ponder the value of the craft itself, both historically and in my own time, and give thanks to Elizabeth Zimmermann, the woman who gave knitters the power over their own creations. I think about the way knitting brings together people of all races and classes and remember the yarn shops that have provided refuge and friends during difficult times in my life. My musings aren't always serious. I often laugh at them the way I laugh as my yarn stash expands, despite my attempts to contain it, and the mental contortions I have to go through to give yarn away.

I share these thoughts with you here, just the way I'd offer you a scarf. If you like them, keep them. If they're not to your taste, pass them on to someone else. That's the nice thing about knitting: it encircles you, no matter which side of the needles you're on.

*Elizabeth Zimmermann*
*Mother of the Craft*

## *Elizabeth Zimmermann* ▬▬▬
### *Mother of the Craft*

At times, small events remind us that creativity not only endures but expands to touch and inspire others. That's why the death of renowned knitter Elizabeth Zimmermann in 1999 was worthy of an obituary in the *New York Times*. Non-knitters must have been confused when they picked up the paper that day. The nation's paper of record devoted almost a thousand words to commemorate the accomplishments of a professional knitter—yes, that's what she was; no, the designation wasn't a contradiction in terms.

Zimmermann wasn't strictly a fashion designer, even though thousands of women and men still follow patterns she created almost half a century ago.

She didn't have the celebrity of the Missonis, the Italian family whose knitwear sells for thousands of dollars, nor the cachet of Kaffe Fasset, the British designer whose beautiful colors turned knitted sweaters into artistic canvasses. Zimmermann had a single-minded passion for the craft that allowed her to "see knitting in everything" and a gift to help others see as she did. By overturning the traditional approach to knitting with her revolutionary techniques, knitters were given the freedom to create patterns to suit themselves.

Her most famous "unvention," which was what she called the techniques she devised, was her method for making a sweater. First, she abandoned straight needles for circular ones. By knitting cylinders instead of flat pieces, she eliminated the need to sew a sweater together. "The human being is so constructed that it [*sic*] can be completely covered by a series of shaped tubes," she explained in her book *Knitting Without Tears*. "We knitters can fabricate natural-born tubes by the very nature of our craft of circular knitting. . . . It is only a matter of uniting the tubes by knitting together and we could, if desired, make long johns for an octopus."

Then she used mathematics, a subject long deemed too weighty for women of her era, to devise formulas that guaranteed a perfectly fitting garment. The knitter determines the number of stitches for the body by knitting a four-inch swatch and measuring the number of stitches that equal one inch. Then she multiples that figure by the desired width of the sweater.

The next step involves following percentages that Zimmermann had carefully worked out. If the knitter wants long sleeves, she casts on 20 percent of the body stitches per sleeve. She increases regularly until she has 33 percent of the body stitches.

After knitting the sleeves and the body, the knitter can relax.

"Now the long haul is over, and the fun begins," Zimmermann wrote. The knitter follows the rest of Zimmermann's directions for joining the sleeves and body by knitting all three pieces together on a circular needle. She guides the knitter step by step from the yoke to the neck, giving percentages as signposts so the knitter won't get lost.

This "unvention" allows a knitter to modify a basic design to her taste by adding small patterns, switching yarns, or changing stitches, without worrying that the finished garment would hang from her shoulders like a sack or squeeze her chest like a vise.

Zimmermann's initiation to knitting was hardly exceptional. She'd been drawn to the craft as a child in England. Her memories of childhood governesses and private schools evoke scenes from a nineteenth-century children's novel—with a daringly modern heroine. "I had a wonderful hidey-hole in a gone-to-seed cabbage patch," she recalled in her book *Knitting Around*, "and one day had the excitement . . . of falling through the roof of an abandoned chicken house, garnering the first permanent scar on my leg."

Surrounded by knitters, one day little Elizabeth asked to learn. Her mother promised to teach her—if she behaved for a full day. The little girl did, and her mother was true to her word. Thus, the course of Zimmermann's life was set. She spent the rest of her life with needles in her hands and yarn looped through her fingers.

She attended art schools in Switzerland and Munich. In Munich she met Arnold Zimmermann—whom she dubbed her "Old Man"—who could "carpenter, plumb, read . . . brew beer, and fish. . . ." They fled Germany after he was heard ridiculing Hitler, married in England, and, in 1937, immigrated to the United States. Eventually they settled down in an old schoolhouse in Wisconsin. Through it all Zimmermann knitted.

As her passion for her self-described obsession deepened, so did her exasperation with the patterns of the day. They were rigid, as if pattern designers were drill sergeants and knitters were new recruits going through boot camp. There was no room for creativity. No room for a woman—because virtually all knitters then were women—to express herself. The message was clear: the knitter—the woman—was supposed to follow, not lead, because the designer—the authority—knew best. But Zimmermann had an artist's eye and the assurance to strike out on her own. Instead of following directions, she modified them and ended up creating her own patterns. She broke ranks and showed others how to do the same.

Am I veering into a feminist interpretation of Zimmermann's life? Yes I am, even though Zimmermann's books suggest she didn't have much to do with feminism. When explaining her Pi shawl design, for example, Zimmermann said, "If you are a man, you probably realize that this is simply the formula for Pi, but if you are a woman, you put such concerns out of your mind when you left high school."

Perhaps she misunderstood the movement. She was a wife and mother, occupations that, at the time, laywomen believed feminism looked down upon. True feminism values a woman's work, as well as a woman's ability to think for and to assert herself. Feminism champions empowerment, a word that didn't even exist in the mid-1950s, when Zimmermann published her first knitting pattern.

When her first pattern appeared in *Woman's Day* magazine, Zimmermann didn't receive a dime.

Instead, the magazine published her name and address as the source for the yarn and patterns. The arrangement was a fair bargain for the time, when a woman's work was undervalued at best and trivialized at worst. Still, it illustrated a law of capital that gave rise to the women's movement in the 1970s: payment indicates value. In the 1950s, society considered women capable of managing a house but not a business. They were to be satisfied with recognition and emotional currency perhaps, but not anything Zimmermann could exchange for yarn or needles.

Zimmermann didn't get paid, but she got an opportunity. And she used it. The readers responded to her invitation to create patterns to please themselves, not a distant designer. Torrents of letters arrived. Four years later, she launched her own publication.

So yes, this is a feminist interpretation of a woman who, in all probability, wouldn't have defined herself that way; however, it doesn't matter whether Zimmermann embraced women's lib or scorned it. She opened the door for other women simply by using her strengths and speaking her mind. Most importantly, Zimmermann made the craft of knitting respectable, while keeping it firmly in the hands of its creators. Quilting, embroidery, and weaving have been elevated from craft to art—the result of the women's movement insisting that traditional women's crafts be taken seriously. Society responded, but, ironically, by taking them out of the home, these crafts lost their purpose. Art school quilts hang on the walls of museums rather than lying on the beds of their makers.

But shawls and sweaters don't hang on the walls of galleries and museums. Art schools don't offer majors in knitting. Knitting remains the Cinderella of the crafts movement. A beautifully knitted hat warms its owner's head and brings joy to all who admire it. And the best part is that anyone can learn to create such loveliness—all one needs is a ball of yarn, a pair of needles, a teacher, and some time. Anyone can knit and more and more people continue to do so.

We have Zimmermann to thank for this. She had a passionate desire to teach others the joy of knitting, not its limitations. Her influence expanded the niche for everyone. Without Zimmermann, we might not have the current range of publishers who specialize in various crafts. Kaffe Fassett might have stayed with oils and canvas instead of turning to yarn and knitting needles. Zimmermann "brought intelligence and validity to a craft that had been trivialized as women's work," Linda Ligon, then president of Interweave Press, told the *Times* for the obituary.

At a time when women had far less control over their lives, Zimmermann gave them confidence. She opened a way for an ordinary woman to enrich her own life and the lives of others. She paved the way for hundreds of thousands of knitters, men and women, to express themselves without relying on an outside authority's approval or oversight.

As the editors of the *Times* rightfully recognized, hers was more than an accomplishment. It is a legacy.

## The Busy Woman's Möbius Scarf

Most knitting references give two ways to knit a Möbius scarf: a method that knits in the round and another that knits back and forth. The first method is so complicated my head hurt when I tried to visualize the process. I didn't dare knit it; I was afraid I'd end up with a tangled mess.

The simpler way involves knitting a scarf, putting a half-twist in it, and then sewing the ends together. The half-twist lies flat when you wear the scarf and it fits wonderfully under a coat or jacket.

My way is even simpler. I use size-17 needles and two strands of yarn and cast on enough stitches for the *length*. Then I knit a few rows—no more than 20—for the desired *width*. Don't be alarmed by the number of stitches. You can make this scarf while watching your favorite television show, and it will be finished before you know it.

I use seed stitch instead of garter stitch to make this scarf. I think seed stitch is a beautiful way to add texture. The pattern is simple: cast on an odd number of stitches, then K1, P1 for every row. Like garter stitch, seed stitch is reversible and the edges of the scarf will not curl.

**Materials:**   2 balls (190–200 yards each) of worsted weight yarn (3½ to 4 oz.)

1 size 17 circular needle

1 yarn needle

**Gauge:** 2 stitches = 1 inch over pattern

**Length:** 60 inches

**Width:** 5 inches

**Directions:** Holding two strands together, cast on 121 stitches.

Knit 1, purl 1 back and forth on circular needles until the scarf is about 5 inches wide. Bind off.

**Finishing:** Put a half-twist in the scarf. Sew the ends together to join the ends of the scarf in a circle.

*The One Who Dies*
*with the Most Yarn Wins*

# *The One Who Dies with the Most Yarn Wins*

I love yarn entirely too much to part with it. I have closets and rooms full of skeins and balls. Sometimes, I even fall asleep while working on my latest project, so I can touch it as I doze. There are times, though, when my ardor cools and common sense reigns. Then I look at my tables and shelves overflowing with yarn. That's when I walk through my house and realize I have to make some difficult decisions.

That is why I sat in the middle of my storage nook, yarn to the back and front of me, yarn to the left (keep) and right (give). I shifted skeins from one pile to another, pausing when I came to the stack of beige cotton.

Should they go to the right or to the left?

I ran my fingers over the tightly plied strands and held a hank up to the light, admiring the way the thread shone underneath the bulb. I'd bought the yarn when I lived in Dayton, back in . . . what? 1991 or 1992? Now it was already well into the twenty-first century, and I lived in Cleveland. The yarn company probably didn't even make that brand anymore; if it did, surely the color had been discontinued.

I'd never started the sweater that had inspired this purchase. For ten years these skeins had waited patiently, expecting that one day I'd actually put my good intentions into practice. I looked at the yarn, humming to myself as I struggled to decide: should they stay or should they go?

I tightened my mouth, turned my head, and tossed them onto the pile to my right, ignoring the twinge of regret and suppressing the tiny thought that still suggested I might want this yarn . . . someday.

"Someday hasn't come yet," I reminded myself. Besides, I was not discarding old yarn. I was *not* admitting that not only had I not finished a project

I'd started, but I'd never started the project in the first place. Rather, I was participating in a meta-physical exercise. I was releasing my hoard to its rightful place in the universe. (Occasionally I have to talk like this to get the job done.)

I perform a version of this ritual two or three times a year. Sometimes I don't toss; I organize. I go to some discount store and buy three or four huge storage containers. I prefer the transparent ones, so I can see my stash at a glance. I sort by color: a layer of reds (cottons and wools); then a layer of oranges (mostly cottons because orange wool doesn't suit my fancy), and finally yellows on top. I push the yarn down so everything will fit inside the bin. Then I snap on the lid and go on to the next assignment: the blues, greens, and purples. Neutrals go into a third bin. The fourth is for variegated and all the other skeins. Then I tote all the bins upstairs to the storage cubby in my attic. I rearrange the bins from the last time I organized and move the trunk filled with yarn back as far as it will go. I put the new arrivals in their place, cut off the light, and close the door. Then I forget about them until the next time I perform the ritual, when I realize that I've once again acquired way too much yarn for my workroom downstairs.

My weakness is as obvious as the balls of yarn decorating my bookshelves, the partially knit hat asleep on my living room table, and the bins stacked in my storage nook. The skeins are more than plied fiber; they are historical markers, detailing the journey of my life. They represent my dreams of beautiful garments and my faith in my ability to create them. Paint dries out, pastels crumble, but yarn lasts for years and years and years. They will be ready when I claim them.

One day I knew I had to make some major decisions. Baskets crammed with wool were pushed under my sewing table. Five tote bags filled with skeins of cotton in blue, yellow, orange, and peach hung from the knobs on my closet doors. I could barely open the drawers of the dresser I'd brought specifically for my stash, and stray balls of yarn sat on top of it. And this was just in the sewing room.

The kicker came when I visited a psychic. This woman had never been to my house and had never met me. In fact, she was in Philadelphia, where I had gone to spend my vacation. She held my hand, closed her eyes, and gave me the first message from her guardian spirits.

"You have a lot of clutter in your house," she said. "You need to clean it up and clear it out to make way for blessings to come."

I didn't need a spiritualist to tell me that I needed to throw out the old and useless and donate the old and usable. But how would I do it?

As I sat in the middle of my yarn, I resisted my impulse to gather up the skeins and hug them like a long-lost friend.

"Be strong," I told myself. "You are releasing this stuff to its rightful place. You are making room for the blessings to come."

Nevertheless, I turned my back to the pile of giveaways. The task would be easier if I couldn't see the growing mass of good intentions.

I picked up another skein of beige yarn. This one was more khaki-colored with a hint of yellow. The giveaways were all cooler shades, perfect for the pale pink yarn I'd bought to match them. The combination reminded me of the beach at sunrise, of the emerging light that tints the sand pale beige here and soft rose there.

The warm khaki couldn't be given away. It was to be married to golden yarn in a sweater or a shawl . . . or something. Really, I hadn't known what I'd planned for the yarn when I bought it. But the colors spoke to me, and I reached for them. So I cocked my head and listened again: which yarn was pleading to stay?

I heard the warm khaki. It seduced me into thinking that I would, *I would*, turn potential into reality. I pushed it back into the storage bin.

The rejects went into a basket I'd brought from downstairs. This yarn was going to a friend of mine, a graduate student whose budget was as much as mine was back in the days when I had paid rent by taking temp jobs and writing press releases. Yarn was a luxury she couldn't always afford. I knew that whatever she took would have a good home.

"These are beautiful," she said as she pulled skein after skein out of the basket. She'd probably expected craft store acrylics and polyesters, the kind of yarn that cuts into your fingers when you push the stitches along the needles.

"I always buy the best I can afford," I said. "You've got to enjoy what you're doing, and that other stuff hurts."

She held up one of the balls of beige cotton. "I bought that yarn in Dayton," I said, beginning the story of my foray into journalism. I told her how I'd moved to Dayton from Mississippi, and to Mississippi from an internship in Cincinnati. By the time she'd picked through the entire lot, she knew everything I'd done for the last fifteen years.

"And what about this?" she asked. She'd switched to a little ball of deep purple tweed. The thread seemed to be solid purple, but the color was deceptive. A closer look revealed thin strands of green and black inserted into the ply.

"I could never make that color suit my skin," I explained, holding out my arm. My dark brown skin seemed to swallow the colors, but the yarn jumped to life when we placed it next to her light brown arm.

I saw a question in her eyes. "Take it all," I urged, "before I change my mind."

I told her the stories of the other skeins. I'd bought the green and khaki tweed in Amsterdam, where my colleague and I had strolled the city's curving streets and come upon a yarn shop. But we had taken a wrong turn on the way back to the hotel and stumbled into the city's famous red-light district. We cringed as we hurried down the street, lowering our heads to keep from seeing the prostitutes exhibiting their wares in the huge display windows. When I got back to America, I hid the yarn in my closet. It had looked so beautiful in the Netherlands, but here I couldn't seem to get it to work with any yarn I had or any I bought. My friend loved it. She gathered it up and set the balls on top of the purple ones.

We drank a cup of tea and talked yarn. We drank another cup of tea and talked about dreams and future plans. I went to find a plastic bag bigger than the one she had brought, and she left with a huge smile on her face.

But her smile wasn't as big as mine. I'd set a goal and accomplished it. I'd exercised discipline. I'd cleaned out my hoard.

I checked the basket. Skeins of red cotton and wool lined the bottom. My friend had rejected this yarn because it was too bright for her taste. They were still waiting for me. This time, I resolved, I will fulfill my intentions. I will make a sweater or a hat or something.

"I promise," I whispered into the basket.

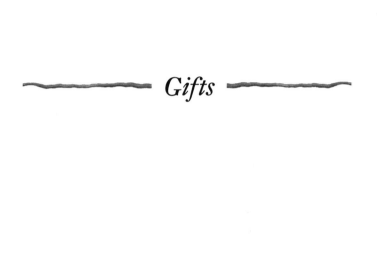

*Gifts*

# *Gifts*

We all know that a teacher can have a lasting impact on a child. How many of us can recall, with affection and clarity, every single detail about the teacher who taught us to read and write, the teacher who believed in us when we didn't believe in ourselves?

As we grow, we cultivate what we learn until it gets incorporated into our everyday lives, until we almost forget that we once didn't know our multiplication tables or how to spell *February*. But sometimes a small event will lead us right back to the days when we sat at our desks and our favorite teacher stood in front of us.

My own journey back started in a most mundane way. I was on the Internet, looking for a slipper pattern I'd knitted as a kid. The slippers were not necessarily beautiful, but soft, warm, and durable. They would be a perfect gift for my husband's ninety-something grandmother.

I found something on my first search and read through the instructions. The pattern called for four ounces of worsted weight yarn and a pair of size-eight needles. My smile grew as large as my excitement. This was the real thing! The size-eight needles were the convincing piece of evidence. My fourth-grade teacher, Mrs. Duncan, had used size eights to teach the class to knit. I looked at the pattern, chuckling over my childhood memories, and suddenly I wasn't a middle-aged writer-reporter with closets full of yarn. I was an eight-year-old, struggling awkwardly with those long, cumbersome needles, trying to sit still long enough to finish a row of twenty-nine stitches. The needles kept falling out of my hands, and the yarn kept slipping off my fingers. Finishing the first slipper seemed to take years. And then I had to make another one.

Yet I did it. And I put knitting down and picked it up again and again from childhood through adolescence, until I finally embraced the craft in my late twenties.

What kept me going back? I've always known that I stay with knitting because I love the beautiful yarns. But that is only part of the reason. I looked at the pattern I'd printed and realized that I stay with knitting because of Mrs. Duncan. I learned a lot from her. She taught me French, and I'm sure that sparked my continuing love of foreign languages. But her legacy, strangely enough, is most evident in the yarns that I collect, the hats that I design, and the books on knitting that occupy an entire bookcase in my crafts room. I wouldn't know how to knit if it hadn't been for Mrs. Duncan.

I hadn't seen her since I was in college, which was almost thirty years ago. I conducted a quick Internet search and found that her telephone number was still listed. My next trip home to Nashville, Tennessee, was just a couple of weeks away. I decided to see her when I got home.

While sitting in Mrs. Duncan's neat study, I noticed that the tops of her tables were clear and each chair sat in a perfect place. The room was so orderly that I wondered if her expertise was in organization instead of teaching. She told me she kept this apartment with an eye toward the future. She was already in her late eighties, she explained, and she didn't want her children and grandchildren searching through her things when she died. So she'd organized all of her belongings and documents, while she was still able.

As she talked, she opened the bottom drawer of her filing cabinet. I looked around the room searching for yarn or knitting needles. Nothing I saw suggested that she was still knitting, but I didn't get a chance to ask her about it right away. The tiny photos she was putting on the table distracted me.

"Do you recognize anybody?" she asked.

I recognized everybody. I had gone to school with them from the fourth grade through the seventh.

Mrs. Duncan and I swapped stories and memories. Ours had been a small, smart, "special" group of kids. I recalled conjugating verbs in French, studying advanced mathematics as well as arithmetic, and belonging to a rowdy class that leapt over the boundaries set for average fourth graders. We had too much energy and too much creativity, and we were crowded into a tiny space. Teaching the class had been a challenge for her and she'd loved it.

"Why did you teach us to knit?" I asked abruptly. I had always wondered whether the knitting lessons were a strategy to calm us down.

"No," she corrected me. "I taught you to knit because you all asked me to. I knitted and I brought some knitting to school. You all saw it and wanted to learn. I always tried to teach you whatever you wanted to know."

Had I wanted to learn French or advanced math? I'm sure I hadn't. I'm not sure I had even *wanted* to learn to knit. It had probably just looked more interesting than set theory, and I'd probably thought I would have a headband if I finished my first project.

But I didn't finish. I could not knit all twenty rows. The headband ended up in my doll's wardrobe, and I'm talking Barbie's collection, not Betsy Wetsy's (the baby doll that wore my mother's handkerchief as a diaper). Looking back, I'm not sure why or how I managed to finish the slippers. The joy of knitting would come years later. My first attempt at knitting was directly related to my love for Mrs. Duncan. If she said that we should knit, I would knit. We both laughed when I told her how hard it was to finish that little headband. We laughed harder when I told her that at the time I'd also forgotten a crucial step in knitting: passing the needle from the right hand to the left at the end of the row.

"I just knitted everything back to the left-hand needle," I said. "I could never figure out why my stitches looked so different from the ones in the pattern books!"

While I was sitting and reminiscing, she pulled out a newspaper clipping about the class. The picture showed the desks arranged in a rectangle, with Mrs. Duncan standing in the middle, where she could walk from desk to desk while facing each student. The reporter had come in time for our French lesson. Mrs. Duncan had just asked a question and three of us were enthusiastically competing to answer. I was in the middle of the trio. Because of my dark skin I was a little blotch in the photo, but I could see that my hand was raised so high that it seemed to pull my body up and out of my seat. I knew the answer and I wanted to be called upon.

I was only eight and I'd already discovered the joy of learning. But joy is too tame a word; learning thrilled me.

Then I remembered another question. "What are you working on now?"

"Oh, I don't knit anymore," she answered.

Mrs. Duncan explained that she had stopped knitting after she'd sent a beautiful blanket to her grandchildren. They loved it, but not as much as Snowball, the family's little dog. She claimed it by climbing onto it at every opportunity, so the family gave it to her. When she died, the blanket was carefully, lovingly folded up and put away.

"I was so mad that they gave my blanket to a dog that I just stopped knitting," Mrs. Duncan finished.

"Well, Snowball recognized quality and craftsmanship," I pointed out. "She didn't chew on it or tear it apart."

Mrs. Duncan had kept some of her projects. She brought out a fisherman's sweater that I drooled over. I told her that I'd never had the patience to knit the intricate cables and bobbles that covered the front of those garments. If I ever finished one, I would do just what she had done: wrap it in tissue as a keepsake.

When our visit ended, Mrs. Duncan gave me a tam and made me promise to wear it. I'm afraid I haven't kept that promise but I've looked at the hat many times and thought about what she'd really given me: the love of learning and the excitement of discovering a new fact, of developing a new ability.

As she might have expected, I have certainly benefited from learning French and math, but knitting has enlarged my world in a way she couldn't have predicted. My world includes not just friends but strangers who see me knitting and come over to talk.

Knitting is a craft that allows me to communicate with others, regardless of language, race, or class. The ability to use needles and yarn to produce a garment is a skill I share with people everywhere. I have that skill, thanks to Mrs. Duncan.

*The Need to Knit*

# The Need to Knit ━━━━━━

Cleveland's winters are a test in endurance. Snow and ice cover the sidewalks and streets. Clouds conquer the sun, and days are gloomy and overcast.

One particular Sunday I'd had enough of the piles of week-old snow that lingered in gray clumps. I needed color, lots of color, and I needed it quickly. I started my car and headed for the yarn shop. Its light and warmth invigorated me as soon as I walked through the door.

I browsed the bins, dallying over the displays and yielding to the temptation to fondle yarn. I'd been in the store about fifteen minutes when I saw an extraordinary hank of fiber. It was a mix of peach, turquoise, and beige wool and ribbon that reminded me of a summer trip to a South Carolina beach. A single skein would make a beautiful scarf that would be the antidote to the lethargy I fought daily.

"How much is this?" I asked.

The clerk glanced at me. "Twenty-seven dollars." I thought about the car note, the credit card payment, and the utilities. I put the yarn back.

My second choice, an intense combination of indigo and red, cost even more than my first.

I finally left with my selections: a shimmering red Lurex, a bright pink ribbon, a ball of brown ribbon that seemed to glow on its own, and another Lurex that blended silver and pale pink. I'd gotten four balls of yarn instead of one. If I mixed them with yarn from my stash, I could make gorgeous scarves to keep and share.

Still, I looked at the yarn in my little shopping bag and thought about what I'd just done.

I grew up in a time when it was sometimes still cheaper to make things by hand. In my mind, I'd always equated knitting with thrift and productivity.

But that day it occurred to me that the reality is quite different. Whenever I go to a yarn shop, I can count on spending thirty to forty bucks.

Something has happened to knitting. When did the craft stop being a necessity? When did it turn into a luxury—even an extravagance?

I've knitted off and on for forty years, and regularly for more than twenty. I've never knitted because I needed socks or because I needed gloves to protect my hands from frostbite; if anything, it is more thrifty and efficient to buy my winter wear than to make it myself. I have never been in the position of the Scandinavian women who knit while tending sheep or even nursing children. My journals don't contain lists of stockings started or sweaters finished. I never knit while walking, like the pioneers who headed westward in the 1840s. I never knit while studying, like the young women of the 1850s. Such women were the original multitaskers. They found ways to add knitting to an already overflowing schedule because it simply *had* to get done—and so did everything else. I've knit for most of my life, but there has never been a time when knitting was work or even considered a way to fill empty hours with industry.

These days, a person who knits is seen (by non-knitters) as doing nothing or having nothing better to do. An office supervisor once taught me this lesson. I was working on a temporary assignment and I'd finished all my tasks that were supposed to last all day. The rest of the workers were busy, so I pulled my knitting out of a desk drawer. I'd gotten a row or two done when the supervisor came over. "It looks like you don't have anything to do," she said.

"I don't."

She pointed to my knitting.

"Just put it up," she said.

"You want me to sit here and do nothing?"

She thought a moment. "You could talk to your friends on the telephone."

I thought the incident was isolated until I read an essay written by pediatrician Perri Klass. Something similar had happened to her when she was a resident. She, too, had been told it was better to look busy than to actually be busy, if being busy meant knitting.

The point is clear: knitting is not work. It is relaxation or even meditation (as I argue elsewhere), but it is no longer the practical craft it had been for centuries.

My epiphany led me to *No Idle Hands: A Social History of Knitting*, in which historian Anne Macdonald chronicles the way knitting shifted from necessity to luxury. She points to the Industrial Revolution, first in Britain and then in America.

When British inventor and entrepreneur Richard Arkwright realized his dream of "manufactories"—buildings filled with mechanical textile looms—in the late 1700s, he did more than make himself a fortune. He made manufactured, profitable, and popular cloth. That was the death knell for the male-dominated textile guilds, which had trained craftsmen and set standards and prices since the Middle Ages. But women had always knitted in their homes, and they kept the craft alive.

In 1789 Samuel Slater, who had supervised one of Arkwright's mills, secretly immigrated to the United States to seek his fortune. His intimate knowledge of his employer's machines and organizational methods intrigued investors. By 1793 Slater established America's first waterpowered textile mill. Like his mentor, Slater helped launch a national industry and eventually killed the need for handmade, homespun fabric.

As knitting moved further and further from the center of daily life, its worth lay in the values it represented. In the nineteenth century, those values ranged from industry and thrift to femininity and motherhood. In times of war, taking up needles became patriotic. According to Macdonald, during the shortages of World War II, knitting briefly reemerged as a necessity. Military men needed socks and other comforts to survive on the battlefield, so no one complained when knitters worked on projects at school, at work, or even in church.

This need ended with the war, however, and since then knitting has increasingly become an optional part of daily life, recreational at best, and certainly nothing we do to save money. In the centuries since Slater's looms started America's industrial revolution, affordable knitted goods flood the market while yarn shops have become the craft equivalent of designer boutiques. Even hand-knitted sweaters from South America cost less than the yarn and labor needed to make a similar garment oneself.

We don't have to knit. So why do we? The answer takes us back to the guilty pleasures of the yarn shop. Today's fibers are so hard to resist. They are more than the simple plied, spun wool of years ago. They are made of ribbon or cotton-knit fabric, dyed to match all the colors of the rainbow, then cut into strips narrow enough to knit. They are nubby alpaca and silk. Today's yarns are playful, coquettish fibers. They flirt with your eyes and fingers and seduce you into looking at them, then touching them. We love the way the textures and colors join into unexpected patterns and combinations. We love the way the threads feel as they slip through our fingers. With them we can create unique adornments, one-of-a-kind pieces of beauty.

As lucky owners of hand-knitted goods, we prize these possessions because we want something that distinguishes us from the crowds, something to make heads turn and eyes open wider. We want clothes and accessories to show our individuality, our taste, our ability to recognize and obtain quality.

I saw proof of this firsthand when I began selling my wares at a local farmer's market. The market was well established; it operated from Cleveland's wet, chilly spring through the start of its daunting winter. The customers were loyal enough to endure the weather, and the vendors did well.

But I was an artist, not a farmer. It was the first year the market rented spaces to artisans and I wasn't sure if customers would be willing to pay a fair price for my hats and scarves. The mixed blessing of mass production has made us all accustomed to lower prices for goods, and it's easy for people to forget to calculate the difference.

I crossed my fingers and put up my sign. *Don't knit?* it read. *Don't worry. I do.*

Some folks slowed down to read the sign and then passed over my products. But one woman picked up one of the most colorful hats, a cotton cloche. It wasn't warm enough for winter; it was almost too flimsy for that brisk fall day. But the intense colors enhanced her complexion. The strong red and blue yarn turned her blond hair flaxen. When she put on the hat, the diagonal triangles accentuated the perfect shape of her head.

"Wow," I gasped. "That hat belongs to you."

She nodded, but her eyes were on a scarf that looked like a fuzzy rainbow. I'd knitted it with one of the new eyelash yarns. When she wrapped the scarf around her neck, passersby stopped and nodded their approval.

"How much?" she asked.

"The scarf is fifty," I said somewhat apologetically. "The hat is thirty-five."

"So it's eighty-five?"

I held my breath as she counted out the money. I opened a bag. She gave me the scarf to put into it, but she wore the hat as she walked away.

That customer taught me that people are willing to pay for something special. She could have bought a silk scarf at a store, but anyone can do that. And while a machine-made silk scarf may be a find, a handmade silk scarf is a treasure. Garments made by hand are more precious because we value the time that went into making them. Silks and other fibers that once indicated status and exclusivity may not be as rare as they were even decades ago and many of us are prosperous enough to spend twenty dollars or more for relatively few ounces of yarn. But *time* is another matter.

Many women work two jobs: They spend their days in an office and go home to tend to their own lives. Meals must be cooked, clothes must be washed, carpets have to be vacuumed, and floors must be mopped. And who is picking up the children? Knitting, no longer an activity performed along with other work as it had been in days gone by, has become a rare treat. Who has time to spend on a sweater? Who has time to sit at all?

Time is a luxury and handmade garments are luxuries, too. But that does not mean that they are frivolous. They are the proof that someone—a living person, not a machine—stole a few minutes here and there to dedicate herself to making a scarf or a sweater. Now, more than ever, knitting is a way to touch others. It isn't a necessity and hasn't been for a long time. But we need knitting, and that makes it invaluable.

## The I-cord Lariat Necklace

This pattern was inspired by all the small skeins of metallic yarn I'd seen in yarn shops. Strangely enough, the yarn brought to mind the knitted, beaded purses I'd seen in antique shops. I admired the tiny bags because they were so luxurious and intricately made. I didn't have the patience to make one myself, but I wanted to knit *something* to display the yarn. I realized it could stand on its own as a beautiful necklace. I used Elizabeth Zimmermann's I-cord technique to knit a long rope, and attached head cones to hide the ends.

Just drape the rope around your neck and secure it by tying an attractive knot. Let the ends dangle.

**Materials:**  20–24 yards of Lurex or other metallic yarn

2 double-pointed needles, size 6

2 head cones

2 beads, size 6°

1 plastic dental floss threader

1 size D crochet hook

**Directions:** This necklace is knit by holding two strands of yarn together. Leave a tail about 5 inches long and cast on three stitches.

*Row 1:* Knit

*Row 2:* Switch needle to left hand **but do not turn the needle!** Instead, slide the stitches to the top of the left-hand needle and knit back onto the needle in the right hand. By pulling the working yarn from the end of the row and knitting into the first stiches, you will make a tube.

Repeat rows 1 and 2 until the tube measures at least 20 inches.

**Finishing:** Cut the yarn, leaving a tail of yarn about five inches long. Thread the tail through the remaining stitches and pull tight to close.

Put the tail through the loop of the dental floss threader and secure to the threader. Pull the threader through a head cone, through a bead, and back through the small end of the head cone. Untie the yarn from the dental floss threader and gently tug the tail until the tube fits into the wide end of the head cone and the bead sits at the top of the cone.

Use the crochet hook to weave the rest of the tail through the stitches of the tube.

Repeat on the other end.

*Ties that Bind*

## *Ties that Bind* ━━━━━━━━━━

One of my joys in knitting is the gift of knitting: a hat made for a friend who just adopted a baby; a scarf for another friend who calls me every day, even though she lives in Missouri and I live in Ohio. While I knit, I remember conversations and situations. Memories and emotions flow from my heart, through my fingers, and into each stitch. The result is a small embodiment of my relationship with the recipient that I can offer as a loving keepsake. It takes a while for me to send the gifts off, though. I like to let them sit around the house. It's as if my friend or loved one is there with me in spirit, if not in flesh.

That's why I was so in love with a black and white cotton pillbox hat I once made for someone. The brim resembled an inverted piano keyboard (the black keys were on the bottom instead of the top). The design was stunning, as unique as a signature.

The design was, in fact, a signature of a woman I'd known only briefly, a woman who can't read or write, but whose art and skill have carried her reputation from her village in Mali across the Atlantic to the United States. Her name is Madame Nakunte Diarra. My hat, and others I have made like it, is a manifestation of my appreciation for the impact she has had on my art.

Madame Diarra doesn't knit; knitting isn't an African craft. Her specialty is *bogolan*, patterned cloths made by applying fermented mud to strips of specially treated handwoven cotton. Bogolan artists often collect the mud a year before they plan to use it. The designs they outline onto the cloth aren't random doodles; they have been passed down for generations and refer to proverbs or historical events. The mud, which is rich in iron and other minerals, resembles a thick, black paint. Masters like Madame Diarra know how to mix the mud so that it produces a warm opaque color. But Madame Diarra is a cultural treasure as well. Her cloths boast symmetrical designs with neat, sharp lines separated by brilliantly white negative space. She never signs her work, but its quality is unmistakable.

Madame Diarra's work hangs in the *African Voices* exhibit in the Smithsonian's Natural History Museum. I met the artist in 1994, when she came to Cleveland for a month of lectures and workshops. Madame Diarra doesn't speak English; during the visit, a translator bridged the language gap that separated her from her audience. But her warmth and friendliness drew us all close to her.

When I began the hat, nine years had passed since Madame Diarra's visit. As I cast on the first round of stitches, I imagined her sitting in front of me and asking about my work. Madame Diarra could have been one of my relatives. She has the same deep brown skin as the women in my father's family, and like us, she has a red patch on her lower lip. While we aren't blood relatives, we have an artistic kinship: we are women who insist on finding time for our craft.

Traditionally, bogolan was made only by women who belonged to a certain caste. The women made the cloth during the dry season, a time when farmers like Madame Diarra weren't busy producing crops. Still, bogolan had to wait until after the cooking and cleaning were finished. But the cloth is important to the society as it is used for rites of passage such as female circumcision ceremonies. Madame Diarra's reputation had spread so far that making the cloths had become an occupation. Even then, she couldn't escape her daily chores, so she essentially worked two jobs.

Madame Diarra didn't tell us this; we saw it in a documentary about her. In it she sits in a yard working and complaining she'd never be able to finish her orders. She fusses about not having helpers, about being expected to do everything for everyone. It was a tirade uttered by women around the world. And through it all, she repeatedly dips a miniature spatula into a pot of mud. Then she presses the pigment into the cloth that lies in her lap. Her motions are quick and sure, almost mocking the lament that had fallen from her lips. She can't stop; she has too much to do.

As I learned more about bogolan and Madame Diarra, I couldn't help but compare her dedication to her craft with my dedication to mine. True, knitting is my hobby, not my livelihood. But how many times have I sealed my latest project in a plastic bag and put it in my purse so I could knit on my lunch hour? How many times have I stopped by the yarn shop to chat when I had free time between meetings? How many times have my fingers moved of their own accord, manipulating stitches and needles while I concentrate on finding the right words for my latest article? How many times have I complained about having too much to do and not enough time to do it, about being there for everyone else when no one was there for me?

I thought about those things and more as I worked on the pillbox hat.

I hosted a party for Madame Diarra when she came to Cleveland. I'd made peanut butter stew, a staple in her country. When she and her son walked into the house, they smiled widely, surprised by the aroma of food from home. But I had another trick up my sleeve. After I checked my pots, I went out to say hello. I'd worn my favorite African dress, a green floral print with white eyelets around the sleeves and yoke. I wasn't the only African American wearing traditional clothing, but I was the only one wearing a dress exactly like Madame Diarra's. I had known we shared the dress because I'd seen her wear it at one of her first lectures. She looked at me and started to laugh. She'd traveled across an ocean to meet a woman dressed exactly like her!

The evening transcended whatever barriers lay between us. Whenever she saw me after that, Madame Diarra gave me a hug and a kiss. And she saw a lot of me. I figured I'd never get another chance to meet an artist like her, so I attended as many of her lectures and workshops as I could.

Madame Diarra was a link to a culture that could have and might have been mine. Slavery fragmented whole societies and cultures, only to make new ones. Where once we'd been one circle, we are now hundreds, intersecting and sharing. Madame Diarra and I are two of a kind, separated by history and geography but connected by our love of our creativity. When I saw her designs, I translated them into my art. I charted the motifs on graph paper, trying different patterns until I found the perfect one. As I knitted the hat that Madame Diarra would eventually take back to her home, I knew that part of me would return with her to the land of my ancestors, celebrating the meeting that had overcome history.

My hat is in Mali now, after a circuitous journey: I gave the hat to a friend, who passed it on to Madame Diarra. I heard she was pleased by the unexpected gift and promised to wear it often.

I trust she sees the hat for what it really is: a memento of how she touched my life.

## Madame Nakunte Diarra's Hat

I've been designing hats for at least ten years and I don't know how many I've made in that time. This pattern, though, means the most to me.

This is not a project for a beginner. You must be comfortable with changing colors or with Fair Isle knitting and know how to make a right-leaning decrease. The cast-on and decreases are a bit unorthodox, but bear with these directions. The hat is an eye-catcher. Whenever a person sees me knitting the pattern, he or she askes what I'm knitting—and then reserves the hat before I finish the pattern.

*Note:* For the yarn, I recommend a machine-washable acrylic-wool blend.

**Materials:** 1 ball (190–200 yards) of white
worsted weight yarn (3½ to 4 oz.)
1 ball (190–200 yards) black worsted
weight yarn (3½ to 4 oz.)
1 size 6 circular needle, 16-inches
1 pair size 6, double-pointed needles
1 yarn needle

**Gauge:** 6 stitches = 1 inch over pattern

**Circumference:** approximately 20 inches

**Height:** 7 inches
(This hat reaches to the top of the ears. If you want
to make a longer hat, repeat the brim pattern twice
instead of just once.)

**Directions:** Cast on 120 stitches in the following
manner:

1. Hold the strands of both yarns together and
   make a slipknot. Slide both loops onto the

circular needle. The white loop should be to the left of the black loop.

2. Insert the point of the right needle between the black loops, as if to knit. Knit a loop of *white* yarn, pull it through and slip the white loop onto the left needle. There should now be three loops on the needle; white, black, white.

3. Insert the point of the right-hand needle between the newest loops. Repeat step 2 using *black* yarn. There should now be four loops—white, black, white, black.

4. Continue knitting loops in alternating colors, twisting the strands **over** each other as you make the loops until you have cast on 120 stitches.

## Ribbed border:

*Row 1:* Knit 1 stitch white, purl 1 stitch black. Continue in rib stitch until you get to the end of the row. Place a marker onto the needle to signal the beginning of the round and join the stitches, being careful not to twist them.

*Rounds 2–7:* K1 white, P1 black to end of round.

## Brim:

*Rounds 1–2:* Knit even in black.

*Rounds 3–5:* *Knit 3 stitches in black, knit 2 stitches in white; repeat from * to the end of the round.

*Rounds 6–9:* *Knit 1 stitch in black, knit 4 stitches in white; repeat from * to the end of the round.

Repeat rounds 1–9 once more (twice more if you want a hat that covers the ears).

## Decrease for Crown:

*Round 1:* Switch to black yarn. *Knit 8, knit 2 together in a right-leaning decrease. Continue from * to the end of the round (108 stitches).

*Round 2:* Knit even in black.

*Round 3:* *Knit 4 in black, knit 3 in white, knit 2 together in white. Continue from * to the end of the round (96 stitches).

*Round 4:* Knit even, maintaining pattern.

*Round 5:* *Knit 4 in black, knit 2 in white, knit 2 together in white. Continue from * to the end of the round (84 stitches).

*Round 6:* Knit even, maintaining pattern.

*Round 7:* Switch to black yarn. *Knit 5, knit 2 together. Continue from * to the end of the round (72 stitches).

*Round 8:* \*Knit 4, knit 2 together. Continue from \* to the end of the round (60 stitches).

*Round 9:* \*Knit 3 in black, knit 2 in white. Continue from \* to the end of the round (60 stitches).

*Round 10:* \*Knit 2 in black, knit 1 in white, knit 2 together in white. Continue from \* to the end of the round (48 stitches).

*Round 11:* Switch to white. \*Knit 2, knit 2 together. Continue to the end of the round (36 stitches).

*Round 12:* Switch to black. Knit even, switching to double-pointed needles if necessary.

*Round 13:* Switch to white. \*Knit 1, knit 2 together. Continue from \* to the end of the round (24 stitches).

*Round 14:* Switch to black. \*Knit 2 together. Continue from \* to the end of the round (12 stitches).

*Round 15:* \*Knit 2 white, knit 2 black. Continue from \* to the end of the round.

**Finishing**: Cut the yarn, leaving a 4-inch tail of both strands. Weave them through the last 12 stitches and pull tight to close. Use a yarn needle and sew the tail into the stitches on the wrong side of the hat. At the bottom of the hat, weave in the tail to close the gap at the cast-on edge.

# *Yarn Shops I Have Known and Loved*

## Yarn Shops I Have Known and Loved

I didn't have plans to knit when I walked across the threshold of Rhode Island Needleworks. I was just curious. I hadn't knitted since high school, when I'd made a sweater for a classmate and only charged her a dollar. My mother had yelled at me for a half-hour; she had been so shocked that I'd placed such little value on my work. Once upon a time, I crocheted but stopped during my freshman year in college. That was in 1971, at the peak of the granny square craze. I crocheted so many hats, halters, and ponchos that I burned out. I crammed all of my handiwork into a bottom drawer. I couldn't bear to throw the stuff out, but I couldn't stand to wear it. I hauled everything from dorm to dorm until I finally ditched it my senior year.

So I wasn't a total stranger to yarn but I'd never seen a shop like Rhode Island Needleworks before. I didn't know that knitting had also crossed a threshold in the decade since I'd abandoned it. European and Japanese yarn manufacturers were creating exotic blends of natural and synthetic fibers, and suddenly knitters could choose between the wool they had used for years and combinations that included fibers with polysyllabic, scientific-sounding names such as polyamide. Skeins might have cotton and linen mixed together; even silk was plied with wool.

And the colors! The blues were so deep and rich, I wanted to take off my shoes and wade into the bins. Another skein looked like a summer sunset. I'd been brought up on evenly dyed, evenly spun strands of yarn. In these new skeins, a single strand might be thick and another might be so thinly spun that it seemed it might break if someone dared to use it.

I had a few dollars on me and a checkbook in my purse. The question wasn't whether I would buy; it was how far I could stretch the money I had. The owner watched me wandering from bin to bin, trying to settle on my first purchase. Really, I wanted everything I saw. We struck up a conversation and when I left, she knew that my name was Afi and I knew that her name was Peg and that her partner's name was Margie. We became friends on that first meeting, and we stayed friends until I finished graduate school three years later.

It took me years of packing my hoard of yarn and carrying it from place to place to understand why Rhode Island Needleworks played such an important role in my life. From Rhode Island to Charlottesville for my first teaching job at the University of Virginia, then to Richmond, Virginia, where I began my writing career, to Washington, D.C., where I got my first full-time newspaper job, and to Cincinnati, where an internship at one of the city's daily papers prepared me for a move to Jackson, Mississippi, all my yarn came with me. From a closet in Dayton to the attic of the house I bought in Cleveland, the yarn from Rhode Island Needleworks has accompanied me along my life journey. In every new town, I found another yarn shop, and in every yarn shop, I found a friend—just like when I wandered into that first store in Providence. Rhode Island Needleworks helped me overcome the loneliness I felt back then. Yarn shops have been my anchor ever since.

To the uninitiated, a yarn shop is just a place to buy yarn. Anyone who has practiced the craft—and here I mean "practiced" in the sense of regularly taking up needles and yarn, the way a musician regularly plays his or her instrument—knows that a yarn shop is more than a retail establishment. For if knitting is a respite, then a yarn shop is a refuge. It is a social center, a place to linger and talk while considering colors and textures and resisting—then yielding—to temptation. A yarn shop isn't a place to do business in a hurry. It's a place to tarry and, inevitably, to spend more money than you'd planned.

I'm convinced that yarn shops are restorative. From that first experience in Providence, I've found that when I'm in a gray mood on a gray day, the hues and shades of yarn lift my spirits. I don't think I'm alone in feeling this way. I've been in too many yarn shops and seen too many customers caressing the yarn to think this is my idiosyncrasy. They, too, walk from bin to bin, stroking the threads while envisioning the beauty they will create. It's as if the balls of wool smother the worries of the day.

And at those times in my life when I have stood at a crossroad, I have regained my sense of direction by thinking, meditating, and hanging out in yarn shops. They are places to go when I know nowhere else to go, places to find friends when I have none.

Almost a decade after I found Rhode Island Needleworks, another yarn shop served me well when I moved to Mississippi. I'd been bred, if not born, in the South and I considered myself a native. But Mississippi is a society and land in itself. I soon learned that I was a child of the New South. I'd seen college students protesting segregation at Nashville's lunch counters in the 1960s, and my family had participated in the boycotts that led to the city's integration. After moving north, I'd become accustomed to going wherever I wanted, whenever I wanted, especially after attending college in Chicago and graduate school in Providence. I'd known prejudice and discrimination but never felt that I couldn't overcome them.

But I found that deeply rooted racial divisions still existed in Mississippi, even in the 1980s. The world was separated into "theirs" and "ours," and the split appeared in ways I'd never expected. This was the state where public school systems held separate, private proms rather than risk the chance that black and white students might dance with each other. In other places where I'd lived, my friends had always come in all colors, both genders, and various sexual orientations. We met for coffee; we called each other to gossip. In Mississippi, blacks and whites only socialized at work. Afterward, we went our own ways.

I tried to understand this code. Wherever I went, I found myself wondering, "Am I the first . . . ?" and "Am I the only . . . ?" Would I be treated with the casual civility that signaled acceptance, or with the formality that meant I'd wandered into an area where I didn't belong—or, rather, wasn't wanted? Thoughts of race infected every decision I made. So I paused a second before I stepped into Celita's yarn shop. Then I opened the door to a warm "Well, how are you?" My reply was met with a friendly "And what can we do for you today?"

"Well . . .," I began, releasing the breath I hadn't realized I'd held.

Celita's specialized in supplies for needlepoint and embroidery. The store featured a small selection of knitting yarns, but it had none of the wool and wool blends I'd seen elsewhere. There was no need for them. Mississippians barely know cold; they shiver when the temperature drops near freezing. While I lived there, my New England sweaters spent most of the winter hanging in the back of my closet. Celita's carried cotton, rayon, and even silk. Knitting with new yarns meant I had to learn new techniques, and that was my reason for stopping by the shop each Monday on my day off.

I could always count on a sincere "Hey, Afi," with the accent on the first syllable of my name instead of the proper way, on the last. I would answer with a "Hey!" of my own, followed by "How y'all doing?" The tempo of my speech would slow and I would sound like the Southerner I was, confident that these folks, unlike my Northern friends, would not pass judgment on my accent. I could let down my guard a little. I could reveal parts of my life and personality. And, in turn, the people in the store could be themselves. One of the salesclerks was from New England. She was a classical musician who played in the symphony with her husband. Her speech sounded stiff and sharp against the smooth, slow sentences that surrounded her. I understood her sense of isolation. Hadn't I been in the place she'd called home, struggling to make myself understood there, the way she was doing here? But at Celita's, she didn't need to moderate her Boston vowels and *r*'s any more than I needed to worry about my color.

Washington, D.C., was the site of the next yarn shop that played a significant role in my life. Each neighborhood in D.C. seemed to have a center where residents, and sometimes tourists, gathered to eat and shop, to see and be seen. I had visited Dupont Circle before and sought it out as soon as I moved to D.C. Dupont Circle had everything I loved: a bookstore with a coffee shop that was really a singles' bar, a bead store, restaurants, and take-out spots. Street performers and vendors brought energy to the scene. But none of these attractions could match the Woolgatherer, a yarn shop right in the neighborhood. The store was in a white house on 21st Street, Northwest. The building contained two businesses. The knitting store was downstairs, to the right as you walked into the foyer. Needlework supplies were upstairs.

I liked the place as soon as I walked in. The renovations hadn't obscured the original layout of the house. The knitting yarns were located in a large front room that had probably been the parlor. The other room behind it looked like a dining room. There was a tiny bathroom at the back of the first floor. I wondered where the kitchen had been.

The owner kept an eye on me as I wandered around, always a step or two away from a purchase. Successful shopkeepers must balance reserve with friendliness. They have to be approachable but not overbearing, reserved but not aloof. This man had just the right touch. He let me wander but always seemed to be nearby when I lingered over yarn. Finally, my dillydallying pushed him over the edge.

"Do you know what you're looking for?" he asked.

"Nope," I admitted.

"Well, what are you working on?"

"A sweater . . . well, really, nothing. I just figured I'd look around and something would come to me."

I held up a skein of cotton. The yarn made me think about a field of wheat shimmering in the midday sun. I'd never seen a field of wheat but I'd seen crops ready for harvest. I thought of the cycle of sowing and reaping, of planting seeds and tending them to ensure a bountiful yield.

I put the skein down and reached for another. I was in Washington breaking ground for a new life;

I was ready to reap some rewards for all of my hard work in Mississippi. I'd pulled as much as I could from my life there and it was time to take all I had learned somewhere else, somewhere I could explore all the facets of my creativity. I just didn't know where that place was. I had no particular city or newspaper in mind, but D.C. was a good starting point. I was browsing, the same way I did in yarn stores, looking at possibilities like I looked at skeins of wool, hoping I'd recognize what I needed when I saw it.

That is why I spent so many Saturdays at the Woolgatherer. I couldn't make a firm decision about my life, but I could pick yarn. I couldn't change jobs—yet—but I could start a new sweater. I could knit the back, then the front, and finally the sleeves, all the time knowing that I was working toward a goal. In the end, I'd have something to show for my efforts. If I were patient, perhaps the same thing would happen with my career and I'd end up with not only a beautiful sweater but a more satisfying post.

The lack of attention paid to my Southern roots while I lived in D.C. was another of the Woolgatherer's appeals. Charles, the owner, never mentioned my accent, which was thicker after my time in Jackson. My other Washington friends laughed at me. Other Southerners had wiped every trace of their nativity from their speech; those from other parts of the country pointed to my accent to justify their stereotypes of Southerners. I'd gotten used to strangers asking where I came from and was a little defensive about it.

One day Charles was helping me kick around ideas for a stitch combination inspired by my Southern background. Following the model of Irish knitters I'd read about whose work was inspired by Irish terrain and culture, I wanted to create a pattern that would give the impression of black-eyed peas and rice, a staple of Southern cooking. After we had thrown ideas back and forth for a while, I jokingly said, "You know what? I'd really like to figure out a pattern called 'yellow-meat watermelon.' But I'd probably have to switch from stitch patterns to using color combinations for it to come out right."

Charles laughed. "Now I know we were supposed to meet." He said his grandfather had developed the variety of fruit.

I nodded. And smiled.

A yellow-meat watermelon is the size of a basketball but sweeter than its larger cousin and lacking in the seeds that make eating watermelon such a tedious affair. Northerners—that is, anyone who isn't from the South or hasn't lived there— weren't familiar with the treat at that time. It was, at least back then, proof of a regional pedigree, like eating fried chicken and gravy for Sunday breakfast or rice with sugar and butter as a side dish for dinner.

Right then, I realized that Charles' speech and his shop was my home away from home, a home until I found my home. The Woolgatherer was a refuge, just as Celita's and Rhode Island Needle-works had been. In these stores I was able to both be myself and lose myself.

In yarn stores, knitters can concentrate on fibers and colors. We can fail without fear. After all, a wrong stitch can be unraveled and reknit. A flawed sweater can be set aside until we decide to pull it out and fix it. There are no penalties to face, no responsibilities to fulfill, no reputations to uphold. We don't make life-altering decisions. We just knit.

That is why yarn shops are such wonderful places. When I walk into one of these stores, I am a woman who belongs to a community that stretches around the world and welcomes whoever wishes to join. In a yarn shop, I'm accepted for who I am: a knitter.

# Sometimes Knitters Are So Lucky

# Sometimes Knitters Are So Lucky

Sometimes knitters are so lucky. When the world presses in too tightly, squeezing us between our desires and duties, we have a ready escape. We can pick up our yarn and needles. We can bundle our gear in a plastic shopping bag and stick everything into a purse, a briefcase, a desk drawer, or even a glove compartment. Our way out requires little more than sophisticated sticks and string. We don't have to leave the room we're in. We don't even have to move from our seats, although settling into a soft, comfortable chair enhances the getaway. We can knit and escape in plain sight. No one looks askance when we flee the scene by picking up the hobby that gives us room and time to think.

Our more knowledgeable friends shake their heads and get out of the way. They don't even attempt to hold a conversation with us; they know our responses will be a combination of words, grunts, and monosyllables when the knitting pulls our attention away. They struggle to clear a path among the balls of yarn, all the while muttering that we could have, at least, finished the shawl before we started the sweater that we put aside when we decided to make hats and scarves for the winter.

We laugh and agree, too content to explain how yarn sparkles like emeralds and sapphires. The wool seduces us and we bask in the colors that lie at our feet.

We laugh and promise to finish whatever project hangs on our needles. And then we'll get to the other stuff scattered around the house. Who believes that vow? We know we'll break it before the words meet the air.

At first, our more sympathetic non-knitting friends look on patiently and smile. "I'll bet knitting is so relaxing," they say, certain that they understand. Then they look at our flying fingers. They see us counting the squares in a pattern and comparing the symbols on the chart to the stitches on the needles. They watch as we unceremoniously interrupt our conversation to correct an almost invisible mistake. This isn't relaxation, they decide. This is stress.

But they don't understand that they were right the first time.

First we concentrate on the pattern and the intricacies written in its instructions. As the piece grows, we slip into the rhythm of our creation. Almost unconsciously, we caress the yarn as it slides through our hands. We finger the stitches, tallying the smooth faces of the knitted ones and the knots at the base of the purled ones. As the piece lengthens from the needle, as sense of peace overtakes us.

Perhaps this is the legacy of our Puritan ancestors: idle hands signal an idle mind, and an idle mind is a workshop for the Devil. For whatever reason, for knitters it is almost unheard of to sit still and do nothing, so we assuage our guilt by reaching for our needles. The pieces of our soul come together and we are whole again.

Sylvia Boorstein, a Buddhist teacher and author, used needlework in her meditation sessions. The first hour of her two-hour sessions was dedicated to knitting, quilting, and embroidering in silence. The second hour turned into a time of talking, not of sweaters and scarves but of worries and fears, of triumphs and struggles.

"Concentration practice strengthens and softens the mind," she wrote in her book *It's Easier than You Think*. One must cultivate the ability to become absorbed in a single activity in order to enter the state that Buddhists call "right concentration." Christians, like the Shakers, also recognize the transcendental power of being consumed by the actions of one's heart and hands.

But popular society scoffs at reflection. We are, after all, the generation that worships the ability to multitask. We steer the car with one hand while we hold the phone with the other. We toss our attention in one direction, then in another. And we wonder why we are so drained.

Knitting is our antidote—at least, for those of us who knit. Just a short time spent absorbed in the touch of the yarn and listening to the click of the needles fortifies and grounds us.

This is what prompts saleswoman Peggy Wilder to take up her yarn in the morning silence while she sits in her Cleveland home, savoring the solitude and warm sun that promises a bright, bountiful day. That day will be packed with sales calls and stops for her business. Her car is her office and she stays on the road. Each morning, though, she stalls those impending demands and takes some time for herself. Her husband has already headed for work when she sits alone with her yarn. She only does a few rows, maybe six, but they are enough to fortify her against the hustle and bustle of her calls and clients.

Peggy Wilder talks like all knitters do. She speaks the language of sweaters knitted years ago and afghans needing to be completed in time for babies' arrivals. These pieces are reminders of deadlines we strain to meet. So why aren't they burdens? Because they are gifts to our loved ones and to ourselves. As we work, the projects magically fill with love that flows from the heart. The magic touches the wearer: the baby sheltered in a blanket or the radiant bride dancing in delicate, lacy stockings. The magic also touches the maker, giving us a glimpse of the divine. We wonder, does God consider Her creations the way we consider ours? Did She start out with a flicker of imagination, a fleeting image that matured into a vision? Did She reach for her favorite tools, the ones that rested most comfortably in Her hands? Did She check them for flaws, was She pleased when She found none, and did She gather them into a circle around Her? Did She settle into the midst of a sanctuary, bending so closely to Her work that it almost touched Her eyes? Did She pour so much of Herself into the work that the creation merged with Her before becoming complete and whole?

What did She feel when She considered what She had done? My imagination gives me a clue.

I believe that She stepped back, surprised by the beauty She had somehow forged. She picked it up and turned it backward and forward, looking for Her imprint. Satisfied that She'd done Her best, a calm pride settled in Her heart before She blessed all She had made and lay down to rest.

*A Knitter's Life*

# *A Knitter's Life* ━━━━━━━━━━━━━━

The bath was supposed to be a relaxing ritual after work, especially on this particular day when I needed to unwind. I'd been on the telephone all day, tracking down sources and verifying facts for an article that was due at 8:15—not 8:16—PM. I'd pulled it off and turned the story in ten minutes early, much to the relief of my equally harried editor. He had rewarded me by letting me go home early.

I tested the water with my toe. The bath was a bit hot, just the way I liked it. I stepped in, sat down, and stretched out until my feet touched the faucet and my chin touched the water. I closed my eyes and thought about a beach with warm sand, where soft waves kissed the shore. I thought about the comforting hiss of the ocean and how I'd loved to be submerged in its waters. I indulged in my little fantasy until the bath water began to cool and my skin began to wrinkle. Then I sat up and, on impulse, decided to examine my breasts.

I usually performed the chore in the shower, but I had gotten lax and skipped a month. It seemed like a good time to get back on track. I carefully fondled my right breast with my left hand, moving in circles from the outside, near my chest, to the inside, near my nipple. I repeated the procedure on my left breast. I'd finished the perimeter when I felt the lump.

It was the size of a walnut. I gently probed the growth, refusing to believe what my fingers were telling me. I repeated the examination again, and again: in the tub, before I went to bed, the next morning when I put on my bra. My fingers always stopped at the lump.

I thought about it at work, when I should have been calling sources. I speculated over its appearance and its meaning in the days leading up to the visit to the doctor's. Still, I wasn't prepared when he voiced my fears.

"This is huge," he said. "You'll have to go to a specialist immediately; this could be cancerous."

He looked at me sternly. "Why did you let this go so long? Why didn't you do regular exams?"

I was too upset to tell him that his receptionist had wanted me to wait three weeks for an appointment, even after I'd told her about the lump.

"I do perform regular exams," I said. "This wasn't there a couple of months ago."

I put on my clothes and went home. That night and the next, I called in sick. I couldn't go to work; I couldn't adhere to the routines that ordered my days. I sat on my couch with my yarn in my lap and my needles in my hands.

What was I making? Who knew? My fingers moved automatically while I confronted my mortality. I was thirty-six. I'd assumed I would live until I was in my seventies; I had relatives who had lived to see their eighties and nineties. Now, just as I'd found my life's path, I was contemplating the possibility of the end of my journey.

What had I accomplished? What would I leave behind?

My fingers manipulated the needles. I'd finished one row and had gotten halfway through another without paying any attention at all to what I was doing.

I took inventory of all my belongings. I didn't have much furniture; it could all fit in a medium-size rental truck. A single trip to Goodwill would clear out the house.

Mama would keep the boxes of books that were stacked in my closet. She'd been a teacher for too long to even consider giving them away, much less consider throwing them away. The clothes would be parceled out to relatives and friends. Anything left would be packed up and—knowing my mother—tossed into the storage shed alongside her house. Then the stuff would mold and rot until someone cleaned out the little building, which wouldn't happen until after Mama died. I smiled in spite of my despair. Mama was such a pack rat; I'd have to rise from the grave and do the job myself.

I sighed. That was everything, except my yarn: years and years' worth of yarn in colors and textures that had inspired the perfect hat or scarf that somehow had never been completed. If I died, whoever cleaned out my house wouldn't see the fabulous sweaters waiting to be created. They'd see balls and balls of beautiful colors but nothing worth keeping in the family.

That's because none of my relatives knit; most of them don't know the difference between a knitting needle and a crochet hook. My relatives would look at my hoard and shake their heads. The piles of half-finished projects would confirm what they'd assumed: I was great at starting things but horrible at finishing them. My family sees my knitting as an out-of-control hobby. How would they know what the yarn and needles really meant to me?

The knitting needles lay in my lap and my hands were still. I'd hoarded my creativity like I'd hoarded my yarn. I hadn't given my love of knitting to anyone. All my teachers—my mother, my grand-mother, Mrs. Duncan—had given me skills that have ultimately enriched my life. They'd done for me what I now realized I wanted to do for someone else. I wanted to pass along a passion, to teach a craft that would be a practical reminder of my life. I wanted to give my family something from my heart, something that could be shared with genera-tions long after my death.

Even after the lump turned out to be a false alarm, this glimpse of mortality left me questioning the choices I'd made in life. While I was happy with my successes—my education, my writing career—so far I had only done things that others might strive to live up to. I still wanted to create a legacy someone could live with—something enduring because it was a constant part of life. That's what knitting was for me.

It's possible to learn to knit from a book, but diagrams can be hard to follow. I've watched dozens of would-be knitters wander into yarn shops, hold-ing a book in one hand and a bag of knitting stuff in the other, searching for help. Knitting is best handed down, or rather, handed across, passed over sets of needles and skeins of yarn. The lessons, formal or informal, build intimacy between the teacher and the students and between the creator and her creation.

But I was the distant relative, the one who popped into Mama's for visits but never stayed more than a week. If I wanted to pass along my love of knitting to the children in my family, I would need time and space to do it. I still haven't been able to surmount these two hurdles, though I came close a few years ago on a visit to my mother's house.

Any adult who visits his or her parents experiences a sense of dislocation. It doesn't matter whether you're twenty-eight, thirty-nine, forty-five, or fifty-one. When you cross the threshold of your parents' house, you're a child. The balance of power shifts in their favor because, subconsciously, you cede your authority. It's their house and you live by their rules. That's why I always pack yarn and needles when I visit my mother. Knitting gives me a sense of place, a connection to the life I've made for myself. My knitting somehow reminds me that I've only come "home" for a visit. Soon I would be returning to my job, my friends, my den where the books stay where I put them, and my kitchen, where my favorite foods fill the refrigerator.

On this particular trip, I especially needed an afternoon retreat. I hadn't gotten much rest the night before. My mother sleeps to the television, turning the volume down to a murmur, but it still woke me up every two hours. At 5:30 AM, the phone rang; the next-door neighbor was calling to wake my mother. He had provided this call throughout the years they taught school and their ritual continued, even though they were both retired.

The calls continued throughout the morning; most folks knew that my mother got up early. In between calls, relatives and friends stopped by to chat. Somehow, I managed to slip away from the action and curled up in the arm of a chaise lounge, knitting and thinking about the path of my life. My solitude didn't last long. My nephew Bakari wandered downstairs looking for me. Even though he was nine,

Bakari made a point of spending time with his adult relatives when they came to visit. I knew it was his way of showing his love and I wanted to encourage it, but I needed the emotional refuge I'd created. I didn't send him away, but I didn't stop knitting.

He sat on the edge of the chaise lounge and pulled two puzzles from the bookcase.

"Let's race," he said. "We can see who finishes first."

But racing puzzles meant I'd have to stop knitting.

"Bakari, I don't want to race," I said. "Why don't we listen to music and talk?"

He negotiated a better solution. We would listen to music, he would play with the puzzle, I would knit, and we would talk.

Our conversation centered on his world: school, games, friends, and all the concerns of a nine-year-old. I commented when I needed to, but I let him do most of the talking. I wanted to stretch this time as long as I could. I knew in a few years he'd be a teenager and his friends would come before me, so I let him set the tone of the conversation.

He played with the puzzle he'd picked for himself, and then he switched to the one he'd brought down for me. From time to time, he glanced at my fingers. I'd finished two rounds before his curiosity got the best of him.

"What are you making?"

"I'm not sure. I think it's a hat."

I'd brought some yarn from my stash and circular and double-pointed needles. I hadn't bothered to make a sample swatch or measure a gauge. This was intuitive knitting, so I picked a number; ninety-six stitches seemed right for a child's hat. I'd knit the brim in rib stitch, alternating scarlet and purple, so the hat would hold its shape. When the stripes grew tall and thin, I'd gotten bored and started making triangles. I held a strand of purple yarn in one hand and red in another. My hands felt so connected to my brain, it seemed that they produced the design as soon as I conceived it. The triangles grew stitch by stitch, round by round.

Bakari had stopped talking. He was staring at my fingers, watching the hat emerge. The expression on his face asked his question before he spoke it. "How do you do that?"

As I prepared to answer, I dropped the scarlet yarn and picked up the gold. In that instant his question changed.

"What are you going to do now?"

"I'm not sure."

Maybe I'd continue with the triangles but switch the order of the colors so that the purple would turn into diamonds. I'd grown a little self-conscious; I wasn't used to knitting with an audience.

Bakari applauded my work by leaning closer.

"Afi, can you knit one for me?"

"Sure. Maybe I'll even give you this one."

"All right."

He got up to leave, then looked at me and put the puzzles back where he'd gotten them. I smiled and he headed upstairs. Soft music and conversation were good, but cartoons on cable were better, I guess.

I looked at the hat and decided to make different one for Bakari. It would be my gift to him. "Maybe one day I will overcome distance and time and pass along the craft," I thought, "but until then I have this hat to remind me of the awe in his eyes, of his thrill at witnessing its creation. This one will be his gift to me."

## Bakari's Hat

This is a variation of the pattern for the hat I gave to my nephew Bakari. I have knit this hat for lots of children since then. I always knit triangles on the brim, but I change the design on the crown so that each child will have a unique version. On this hat, the triangles alternate between dark green, light

green, and purple. For the stripes on the crown, though, I only used light green and purple.

I always use bright colors on these hats because children love them. I love bright colors, too. They make my fingers happy.

*Note:* For the yarn, I recommend a machine-washable acrylic-wool blend.

**Materials:**    Color A = 1 ball (190–200 yards) dark green worsted weight yarn (3½ to 4 oz.)

Color B = 1 ball (190–200 yards) light green worsted weight yarn (3½ to 4 oz.)

Color C = 1 ball (190–200 yards) dark purple worsted weight yarn (3½ to 4 oz.)

1 size 6 circular needle, 16-inch

1 pair size 6, double-pointed needles

1 yarn needle

**Gauge:** 6 stitches = 1 inch over pattern

**Circumference:** approximately 16 inches

**Height:** approximately 7½ inches

**Directions:** Cast on 96 stitches in the following manner:

1. Hold one strand of dark green (color A) yarn and one strand of light green (color B) yarn

together and make a slip knot. Slide both loops onto the circular needle. Color A loop should be to the left of color B.

2. Insert the point of the right needle into the Color B loop, as if to knit. Knit a loop of color A, pull it through and slip the color A loop onto the left needle. There should now be three loops on the left-hand needle: color A, color B, and color A.

3. Insert the point of the right-hand needle into the newest loop. Repeat step 2 using color B yarn. There should now be four loops—A, B, A, B.

4. Continue knitting loops in alternating colors, twisting the strands **over** each other until you have cast on 96 stitches.

## Ribbed border:

*Row 1:* *Knit 1 color A, purl 1 color B. Continue in rib stitch until you get to end of the row. Place a marker onto the needle to signal the beginning of the round and join the stitches, being careful not to twist them.

*Rounds 2–10:* K1 color A, P1 color B to the end of the round.

## Brim:

*Round 1:* *Knit 5 in color A, knit 1 in color B; repeat from * to the end of the round.

*Round 2:* *Knit 4 in color A, knit 2 in color B; repeat from * to the end of the round.

*Round 3:* *Knit 3 in color A, knit 3 in color B; repeat from * to the end of the round.

*Round 4:* *Knit 2 in color A, knit 4 in color B; repeat from * to the end of the round.

*Round 5:* *Knit 1 in color A, knit 5 in color B; repeat from * to the end of the round.

*Round 6:* *Knit 5 in color C, knit 1 in color A; repeat from * to the end of the round.

*Round 7:* *Knit 4 in color C, knit 2 in color A; repeat from * to the end of the round.

*Round 8:* *Knit 3 in color C, knit 3 in color A; repeat from * to the end of the round.

*Round 9:* *Knit 2 in color C, knit 4 in color A; repeat from * to the end of the round.

*Round 10:* *Knit 1 in color C, knit 5 in color A; repeat from * to the end of the round.

*Round 11:* *Knit 5 in color B, knit 1 in color C; repeat from * to the end of the round.

*Round 12:* *Knit 4 in color B, knit 2 in color C; repeat from * to the end of the round.

*Round 13:* *Knit 3 in color B, knit 3 in color C; repeat from * to the end of the round.

*Round 14:* *Knit 2 in color B, knit 4 in color C; repeat from * to the end of the round.

*Round 15:* *Knit 1 in color B, knit 5 in color C; repeat from * to the end of the round.

## Decrease for Crown:

(Switch to double-pointed needles when necessary)

*Round 1:* Switch to color B. *Knit 4, slip 1 stitch onto right-hand needle as if to knit, knit 1, pass slipped stitch over knit stitch (PSSO). Repeat from * to the end of the round (80 stitches).

*Rounds 2–3:* Knit even in color B.

*Round 4:* Switch to color C. *Knit 3, slip 1, knit 1, PSSO. Repeat from * to the end of the round (64 stitches).

*Rounds 5–6:* Knit even in color C.

*Round 7:* Switch to color B. * Knit 2, slip 1, knit 1, PSSO. Repeat from * to the end of the round (48 stitches).

*Rounds 8–9:* Knit even in color B.

*Round 10:* Switch to color C. *Knit 1, slip 1, knit 1, PSSO. Repeat from * to the end of the round (32 stitches).

*Rounds 11–12:* Knit even in color C.

*Round 13:* Switch to color B. *Slip 1, knit 1, PSSO. Repeat from * to the end of the round (16 stitches).

*Rounds 14–15:* Knit even in color B.

*Round 16–17:* Repeat rounds 13 and 14.

**Finishing:** Cut yarn, leaving a 4-inch tail. Weave it through the remaining stitches and pull tight to close. Use a yarn needle and sew the tail into the stitches on the wrong side of the hat.

Weave in all loose strands from the color changes. At the bottom of the hat, weave in the tail to close the small gap at the cast-on edge.

*Beyond*
*Stitch and Bitch*

# *Beyond Stitch and Bitch*

I first heard the term "stitch and bitch" from a coworker who invited me to her home one Friday night. When I got there, she and her partner had already laid out the refreshments: a six-pack of beer and a couple bags of chips. I pulled out my knitting while they sorted strands of embroidery floss until the top of the table looked like an artist's palette. Then they carefully pulled the thread through a large piece of fabric so that each strand surrendered its individuality to form the emerging picture.

They sewed and sipped. I knitted and sipped. Stitch by stitch our handiwork grew. In between we bitched. In the comfort and confidentiality of our surroundings, we three disgruntled employees dished dirt about our bosses. Round and round the tiny circle we went, unloading our frustrations. At the end of the evening, we packed up our stuff, hugged, and parted.

"Damn," I said to myself as I drove home. "I haven't felt this good in a long time."

Without realizing it, I'd been pulled into the intimacy of a craft circle similar to those of the previous generation. But my friends and I weren't that different from our mothers, who met to stitch and bitch during World War II. The topics may have changed, but knitting still belonged to our personal lives, not our public one. Lately, however, I've noticed a generation gap in knitting, a way of doing things that separates the older, more traditional knitters from their younger counterparts. I'm not talking about techniques. Nobody has invented a new way to cast on or bind off. We still pass on and pass around stitches and methods. I'm talking about an attitude toward knitting that has popped up in the last few years as a new generation has discovered the craft. Sure, they embrace knitting because it's meditative and spiritual, because it evokes feelings of home and hearth. They love the way knitters bond over sweaters and hats, the way sharing the craft builds intimacy. They may stitch and bitch like their foremothers, but they've moved beyond the circles where knitters gathered only to share feats and failures. They've decided that the craft has force and energy.

That's why Canadian knitter Grant Neufeld has adopted a ball of yarn with a lit fuse as the symbol of his Revolutionary Knitting Circles. One of his groups took their needles and yarn to a main street in Calgary during the meeting of the G8, the summit of the leaders of the world's major industrialized nations. Miles away in Ottawa, another group joined hundreds of knitted squares to represent the safety net of social services. The participants believed that governmental programs are endangered by calls for privatization, and they were making the clicking of their needles heard.

My friends and I are committed to women's rights, but we had never thought about using knitting to fight the system or gain equality. We probably would have been ridiculed for raising such a notion, and we would have laughed at the thought of needles raised in protest. Peaceful demonstrators held only signs in their hands. Moderate activists changed society by writing to legislators and filing suits. More militant revolutionaries of the '60s and '70s stockpiled guns and bullets, not yarn.

The new knitters see a power in the craft that we had overlooked. The very domesticity of the craft is its strength. How can you subdue a bunch of protestors sitting in the middle of a street, talking and working on sweaters? How do authorities justify breaking up a group of people in the process of creating art?

Neufeld feels that knitting makes provocative statements about the limits of gender and age roles (after all, only old ladies are supposed to knit) while advocating a peaceful, constructive revolution. He believes that knitting is a way to remind people that they do not have to be consumers, that *they* can provide the things they need. "We are creating community and local independence, which, in this corporate society, is a truly revolutionary act," he writes on his Web site.

Lauren Carter, a knitter who lives in Chapel Hill, North Carolina, also sees knitting as a model for nonviolent action. That's why, when she heard about a twenty-four-hour knit-in to benefit homeless shelters, she organized a similar event in her town. She paid for the space and got yarn shops to donate the yarn. Forty knitters came to the event. Other people stopped by to drop off items. The knit-in happened to fall on the same day as a demonstration against the war in Iraq, so, naturally, talk turned to politics. The knit-in hadn't started out as a protest, but the knitters couldn't help but compare their approach to activism with the stance taken by the government. The contrast gave the knit-in a deeper significance, she said.

"Knitting is a nonaggressive act. It was a counterpoint to war," she said.

It's not surprising that politics is often a topic at Lauren's weekly knitting circle. She and her friends are liberal and progressive; the knitting circle gives them an opportunity to discuss and digest current events. "We talk about lots of things: who we like and why we don't like who is in the White House."

The topics may be heavy, but that doesn't mean that the generation doesn't take time to have fun. Lauren assured me that her group also talks about "regular knitting stuff and regular life stuff. We talk about the men in our lives. We discuss new yarns and patterns," she said.

A skeptic may roll her eyes and shake her head. We are talking about knitting here. Can these circles make any difference? Right now, I can't say definitively. But my answer is a hopeful "yes."

For many of these knitters, no matter where they go, knitting goes: to a bar or a party, a meeting or a demonstration. They have taken that 1960s slogan literally—"The political is personal." They still keep the circle but they're also giving the craft a new identity and vitality. The circle has expanded to include both men and women of many ages and cultures. For some, stitching and bitching is a way to take a stand while having a good time. For all of us, it supplies a soothing and inspiring connection to others; we do what we love and we are heard.

 *Redemption*

# *Redemption*

I've seen people knit in lots of places: on the bus, in the park, in a doctor's office, or in a clinic waiting room. People knit in coffee shops, slipping stitches from needle to needle between sips of their morning java. Some of my friends have confessed to knitting while driving. They pick up their project during a traffic jam or when they're waiting at a stoplight. When the cars begin to move or when the light turns green, they lay the knitting on the seat and put their hands back on the steering wheel.

But these are all ordinary, perhaps whimsical, ways of finishing a row or two. I'd never thought that knitting could have a more serious side, that the craft could be a means of rehabilitation, until I learned about an unusual program at the Ohio Reformatory for Women.

At this reformatory, the inmates in one residence hall work on all sorts of needlework projects that are donated to charities and eventually distributed to individuals who need them. The official name of the dormitory is the Washington Residence, but the women housed there have christened it "The Stitching Post."

I'd read about the Stitching Post in a newsletter from a yarn shop. In the article, prison administrators asked for donations of yarn, needles, and other supplies. I sent them some skeins I'd had for years. Then I e-mailed a friend whose mother, once an avid crocheter, had recently died. Her daughters packed up her supplies and mailed them off, confident that their mother would approve of such charity.

Still, the blurb nagged at me. I knitted for many purposes: to make clothes and gifts and even to calm myself and forget my worries. But knitting as atonement? Knitting as a way to pay society for a crime? My journalistic sensor went off. This was a story I couldn't resist. Within a week of receiving the newsletter, I was sitting in the waiting room of the reformatory.

The room was sterile and stern, as if warning the visitor that prison is an institution built on regulations and requirements. Here you will dress a certain way and walk in measured, precise steps; you will eat and sleep at predetermined times; you will leave your cell at three in the morning for the first of six inmate counts. Here your life is not your own. You gave up that control when you committed the crime that brought you to this place.

The guards didn't smile or make small talk; they were there to do their jobs, not to fraternize. As I waited for the public information officer who would be my escort, I pondered the gap between the reality of prison life and the usual connotations of knitting. Something about knitting evokes images of domesticity and femininity. It's a stereotype of course, but one that is attached to the craft so strongly, it seems be spun into the yarn we buy. Something about knitting says warm food and clothes, a woman—usually elderly—taking her rest after tending to her home and family. The craft belongs to the warm-hearted grandmother; it confirms the notion of women as nurturers.

Yet the women's reformatory challenges that idea. The people I interviewed were proof that women can give life and take it, too. And if I dismissed these women by saying that they were hard-hearted and calculating, that they were exceptions, not the norm, then I had to ask them why they, of all women, were doing these crafts.

They didn't hesitate to answer. "The Stitching Post" was their second chance. One woman serving time for robbery, had fallen in love with needlework, a hobby she never would have considered before her conviction. She had never thought she was good with her hands. I watched her nimbly pull her needle and thread through the piece of canvas while she mused about her circumstances. "People think [prison] is inmates banging on steel bars," she said. "It can be that if you want it to be, or you can apply yourself and be positive."

The rest of the group nodded in agreement.

The Stitching Post sprang from the philosophy of restorative justice that is championed by the Ohio Department of Rehabilitation and Correction. Restorative justice advocates more than apprehending and punishing lawbreakers; it seeks to teach an inmate that he or she is accountable to society. Society isn't an abstract notion. It's composed of the offender and his or her family, the victim and his or her family, and their community. "Prisoners have an obligation to their communities," Julie Halyama, a prison administrator, told me in an interview. "Although they've paid their debt to society in terms of the legal requirement, they have things to do in order to earn their way into society's good graces." Those things can be as large as the houses that inmates have built with the Habitat for Humanity programs, or they can be as small as the needlepoint pillows sitting on one inmate's lap.

Several of these women would not live outside the prison grounds for years, if ever. A mother and daughter were serving time for murder. Another woman who sat a couple of chairs away had been convicted of killing her husband. (She was young and pretty; he was old and wealthy. Prosecutors had successfully argued that she had married and murdered him for his money.) Two women had physically abused children in their care. These women all sat in a circle of domesticity, knitting, crocheting, working on needlepoint, and embroidering pillows.

I looked over my shoulder. A guard sat nearby, nonchalantly attentive. I looked back at the women. Each of them wore the institutional uniform of a light green top and a khaki skirt or pants. Was this industrious little scene for show, or were these women really working for another shot at life? Even if their motivation was strictly self-interest, stakes were high: all the residents must spend at least thirty hours a week on their projects, and the women keep time sheets that are checked by the administrators. If a resident misses her quota, she risks being moved from the housing unit. Getting back in would be difficult: there is a waiting list because life inside the Stitching Post is better than life outside. The rules aren't relaxed but the atmosphere is different. "It has helped [our] behavior," one woman said. "People are positive. You see people knitting; you don't see cliques."

I listened and took notes in the special shorthand I'd developed so I wouldn't miss a word. As I bent over my pad, I caught a glimpse of a circle of hands moving steadily, whether pulling needlepoint yarn through canvas or manipulating knitting needles to finish a row.

I am used to knitting at my leisure. It is my reprieve or sometimes my reward for completing a chore. But these women had no time for idleness. It was as if each project proved they could be more than an inmate with a number and a sentence. These women were working for so much, including their self-esteem and the pardon of everyone they'd hurt. These women had a lot to do and relatively little time to make their quota. They were knitting to reclaim their lives.

In their own way, the women were proving a theory made more than a century earlier by the anonymous authors of the *Ladies Work Table Book*. This instructional volume, written in 1845, was aimed at genteel women whose fanciful needlework would strengthen their influence over "the pursuits and destinies of man." The authors warned that knitting and other needlework techniques were not trivial pursuits but the means to a noble end. "Our aim is not to make . . . servile copyists," they preached, "but to lead to the formation of habits of thought and reflection, which may issue in higher attainments than the knitting of a shawl."

No doubt the authors would have been horrified by the deeds of the women in the circle that surrounded me. But I found these women's stories and comments echoing the words of nineteenth-century idealists who insisted that needlework is "capable of becoming an important monitor to the female heart . . . a silent but salutary moral teacher." These women know that their characters are under scrutiny that will be difficult to overcome, but they believe that the mittens, blankets, and hats they produce show the world how inmates can, and do, change for the better.

When I finished asking questions, the women took me to the card table in the corner. The group watched proudly as I counted the items that they had arranged on the table. There were six bed pillows, three stuffed toys, four scarves, six hats, one sweater, five headbands, and a couple of "quillows"—a lap quilt that cleverly folded into a throw pillow.

I shook my head at such productivity and skill. The stitches in the scarves and hats were even and tight. Each item had been carefully and thought-fully made.

"As we finish projects, it's nice to see something beautiful coming out of here," one of the women said. "It puts life in balance."

I weighed her words during the two-hour drive back to my office. Could a sweater or a headband pay for the pain these women had caused? Of course not. What counted was their redemption and their recognition of their debt to society. What mattered was that they had chosen to pay off that debt, one stitch at a time.

# OTHER BOOKS FROM
# BEYOND WORDS PUBLISHING, INC.

## The Letter Box
*A Story of Enduring Love*
Authors: Mark and Diane Button
$16.95, hardcover

Mark Button and his wife Ronnie were eagerly awaiting the birth of triplets when—on Mother's Day—Ronnie tragically died without warning. In time, Mark met Diane through a mutual friend and together they began to build a new life. Desiring to always "be there" for their first child, they started to write her letters—the first within hours of her birth. Mark and Diane have continued this tradition, and now each of their children has a Letter Box filled with special memories and encouragement for the future. *The Letter Box* reminds readers to savor precious time with loved ones and includes instructions for creating their own Letter Boxes.

## The Art of Thank You
*Crafting Notes of Gratitude*
Author: Connie Leas
$14.95, hardcover

While reminding us that a little gratitude can go a long way, this book distills the how-tos of thank-yous. Part inspirational, part how-to, *The Art of Thank You* will rekindle the gratitude in all of us and inspire readers to pick up a pen and take the time to show thanks. It stresses the healing power that comes from both giving and receiving thanks and provides practical, concrete, and inspirational examples of when to write a thank-you note and what that note should include. With its appealing and approachable style, beautiful gift presentation, charming examples, and real-life anecdotes, *The Art of Thank You* has the power to galvanize readers' resolve to start writing their all-important thank-you notes.

## Path of the Pearl

*Discover Your Treasures Within*
Author: Mary Olsen Kelly
$16.95, hardcover

The pearl and its legendary mystical, restorative, and healing powers have ignited imaginations for centuries. *Path of the Pearl* captures the strength of this enduring symbol by using the pearl as a metaphor for personal growth. A pearl oyster, invaded by an irritant it can't expel, turns adversity into a glowing iridescent work of nature's art. This book acknowledges and celebrates the similar path shared by women, particularly in midlife.

## Midlife Clarity

*Epiphanies from Grown-Up Girls*
Editors: Cynthia Black and Laura Carlsmith
$14.95, softcover

The wisdom of a woman is one of our earth's greatest natural resources. *Midlife Clarity* brings together the insights of thirty women from all over the country who have found clarity in midlife and have life lessons to share. Hear their thoughts on the duality of the female nature, vulnerability, body acceptance, freedom, self-discovery, men, the decision whether to have children, and mindfulness of the moment. The diverse entries include essays, humor, personal stories, opinion pieces, and short poetry. *Midlife Clarity* is a timely, touching, and often hilarious window into the hearts and souls of the treasured, yet often overlooked, gatekeepers of the human condition.

## Ocean Oracle

*What Seashells Reveal about Our True Nature*
Author: Michelle Hanson
$24.95, softcover w/ card deck, boxed set

 Combining the ancient art of divination with the mysticism of seashells and their interaction with humankind throughout time, *Ocean Oracle: What Seashells Reveal about Our True Nature* borrows from many disciplines to produce a new and inspiring divination system based on seashells. The boxed set is comprised of 200 full color seashell cards, a companion book, and a four-color fold-out sheet with overview plates of the 200 shells. Appreciation for the shells' aesthetic beauty is enhanced by the text descriptions detailing the animals' behaviors, abilities, interactions with humankind, and their meaning. The shells serve as tools to assist you in revealing subconscious, hidden beliefs and attitudes.

*To order or to request a catalog, contact*

**Beyond Words Publishing, Inc.**
20827 N.W. Cornell Road, Suite 500
Hillsboro, OR 97124-9808
503-531-8700

You can also visit our Web site at *www.beyondword.com* or e-mail us at *info@beyondword.com*.

# Beyond Words Publishing, Inc.

OUR CORPORATE MISSION

Inspire to Integrity

OUR DECLARED VALUES

We give to all of life as life has given us.

We honor all relationships.

Trust and stewardship are integral to fulfilling dreams.

Collaboration is essential to create miracles.

Creativity and aesthetics nourish the soul.

Unlimited thinking is fundamental.

Living your passion is vital.

Joy and humor open our hearts to growth.

It is important to remind ourselves of love.